Failing Heaven

Failing Heaven

Charles Behlen

Copyright © 2014 Charles Behlen
All rights reserved.
Manufactured in the United States of America

ISBN: 978-0-9911074-5-2
Library of Congress Control Number: 2014942296
Front Cover Art: Francisco Goya, "The Dog"
Photograph of Author: Ray Beair

Lamar University Press
Beaumont, Texas

For Laura Belle and Poppa Dave

Poetry from Lamar University Press

Alan Berecka, *With Our Baggage*
David Bowles, *Flower, Song, Dance*: Aztec *and Mayan Poetry* (a new translation)
Jerry Bradley, *Crownfeathers and Effigies*
William Virgil Davis, *The Bones*
Jeffrey DeLotto, *Voices Writ in Sand*
Mimi Ferebee, *Wildfires and Atmospheric Memories*
Ken Hada, *Margaritas and Redfish*
Michelle Hartman, *Disenchanted and Disgruntled*
Katherine Hoerth, *Goddess Wears Cowboy Boots*
Lynn Hoggard, *Motherland*
Gretchen Johnson, *A Trip Through Downer, Minnesota*
Janet McCann, *The Crone at the Casino*
Erin Murphy, *Ancilla*
Dave Oliphant, *The Pilgrimage, Selected Poems: 1962-2012*
Carol Coffee Reposa, *Underground Musicians*
Jan Seale, *The Parkinson Poems*
Carol Smallwood, *Water, Earth, Air, Fire, and Picket Fences*

For information on these and other Lamar University Press books go to
www.LamarUniversityPress.Org

Other Books by Charles Behlen
Texas Weather
Dreaming at the Wheel

Acknowledgments

I am grateful to the editors of the following journals, anthologies, and chapbooks for publishing some of the poems in this book.

Armadillo
Arrowsmith
Borderlands: Texas Poetry Review
Concho River Review
Langdon Review of the Arts in Texas
New Mexico Humanities Review
New Texas
RE: Arts and Letters
Sin Fronteras
Southwestern American Literature
Voices International
Windows
Roundup
Uirsche's First Three Decades
The Voices Under the Floor
Texas Weather

Many thanks to the Texas Institute of Letters and the University of Texas at Austin for a Dobie Paisano Jesse H. Jones fellowship in 1995, and to the Frank Waters Foundation for a fellowship in 1996, during which some of these poems were readied for publication.

Section title credits: (I) Wallace Stevens, (II) Rainer Maria Rilke, (III) William Stafford, (V) Todd Moore

CONTENTS

1   Iron Lung

I. The people grow out of the weather

5   Tishomingo
7   Learning to Fly
8   Water in Armor
9   Summer of '61
10   Love Song for Ray's Exxon and X-rated Arcade
11   Love Means Letting Go
12   Lovington, NM
13   The Pimps Must Be Breaking Arms on Broadway
14   Scene on South Presa
15   My Father Thinks He Lived Once Before
16   Home
17   Raymond's Gone Fishing
18   Homesteading Near Lubbock
20   The Blues
21   Late Summer Comes to Slaton, Texas
24   Weathering Heaven

II. And the animals know we are not at home in our translated world

29   An Uninvited Guest
31   The Charm
32   Here, Boy!
33   The Chimps at Hendler's Welding
34   Cow in the Suburbs
36   Listening to Cattle in the City
37   Age
38   Loneliness at Fort Clark

40 Stepping into a Peepshow at the End of 1977, I Think of Rilke's *Tenth Elegy*

III. Where smoke goes

45 Ballad of the Cotton Compress
47 Called Out
48 When Lewis Punched the Valdez Kid—
49 Range-testing
51 At the Food Bank
52 Ballad of Mackenzie Park
57 On Not Painting Vacant Farmhouses in Sulphur Bluff, Texas

IV. Roads and rivers

61 Halloween on the Serengeti
63 Charlie Parker
65 Inspiration Hills 90
67 LeOta Hodge Talks About Life
69 Nepo Road
71 Let's Go
72 Fjords
73 National Corpse
75 Making 84
77 Agent Orange
78 M.I.A.
79 Highway E90
80 Uirsche's First Three Decades
82 Lake Watauga Drawdown

V. And then night was there

- 87 Everyone Needs a Job. Everyone Needs to Be in Touch
- 89 Hot Day at Hank's Wrecks and Derelict Drive-in
- 91 House in the Country
- 92 Brief Museums
- 94 Watching the Mad Sleep
- 96 The Wall Clock at Miss Edna's Boardinghouse
- 97 Cauthorn
- 99 My Kid Sister and the X-ray Machine
- 100 Failing Heaven
- 102 Burying My Book

Iron Lung

Ensconced in pods,
in the life-giving, coffin-shaped ships,
they lay as in state,

children my age
on display at the Plains Fair
'polio show'—

the mirrors fixed above
each wan face
shaking with the generator's

frantic rattle.
Back on the midway, Dad waved out a match
and sucked in his Winston

while the Ferris wheel and Tilt-a-whirl
churned the crowd up, around,
then dumped them screaming.

Overhead,
Sputnik II swept past
like our TV set in a Texas windstorm—

the small dog Laika
strapped inside.
At school I moped over news photos

of those wild eyes
thrashing in a vacuum
while the older boys pinched

fresh creases in their jeans
and daydreamed up
through cranked-open casements

at skies soon to darken
with the fires of Khe Sanh.
On the nightly news

Khrushchev fired his fat baby's
"We will bury you" grin
straight through our Philco

as the sharp barks
of the collie next door
burst against our den's bay windows

and I breathed in and out
the TV's radiant
Cold War snow.

I. The people grow out of the weather

Tishomingo

Copperheads,
their oiled light,
poured through the brush
as I held each twig
with my breath, waited
for the ancient bass
to break the black pond.
On his sway-backed homestead
Great-grandfather Hodge
worked the slouched
gate of his frame
past Depression headlines
on his newspapered walls,
past the ditched beds piled
with stiff dry wash.
While his son's 10-gauge
bucked in the pines
the squirrels cringed, listened.
As their fat chatted on
the wood-burning stove
I darted into the cold
where the well held
its coin of moonlight.
Dredging it up
with a roped pipe sealed
with a can, I brought
that light to my face, felt
the farm drift through
the Oklahoma dark.

Half a life later,
I returned to find

the house burned flat.
Roaring in his overalls,
someone smashed a flask
on the white rotting clapboard
and the house went up
in one light,
blushed the fields
around Tishomingo.
But the chimney stood
like a well in the air.
I spread my pallet
on rain-pocked ash,
let the unhinged flue
whistle through my sleep.
I dreamed up Hodge's
rocker from the pond
and it shuddered again
in his rapt hands, danced
like a backwoods bride
through the screen door.
The long dead hens, whose
quills walked my back
as I curled by firelight,
stormed my sleep.
The headboards stalled.
The north wall, scored
by lovemaking, flamed.
The knotted wash smoked
and arose like ghosts
while the moonlight reached
down the coked chimney,
stroked my face and raced on.

Learning to Fly

When he saw me, Dale
was working wire straps
through cardboard wings.
He said, *Put them on.*
I acted quickly
as the first March gusts
slapped down the stalks,
slapped them back up
and sent long wrists of dust
searching the turn rows.
My shirttail furious,
spanking my neck,
I staggered forth flapping.
A big gust bent
the creased cardboard down
and I trawled the furrows
on my belly and ass,
came up spitting curses
and cornfield straw.
Then my sneakers broke free
and I treaded the air
for two seconds, three
'til a downdraft slammed me
into a ditch. Righted,
I steadied into the next rise—
the wind wet on my wrists,
Dale far off, calling,
My turn Come back.

Water in Armor

One winter my brother
bandaged like hands
the broken taps

and we hauled water
in heavy milk cans.
Night ice snapped

the bent-down poplar,
bleached the weeds
where a woman was found,

palms up to the weather,
hair starred with seeds,
elbows in the ground.

Boots side-stepped her marker
as we rolled those blunt tin rears
past the wrecks

of another blizzard,
or waltzed them by ears
spot-welded to necks.

The north wind scissored
our deadened crotches,
but we humped those hulks

through a loveless December
of awkward sloshes.
No women, no luck—

just water in armor.

Summer of '61

Dad and I'd stand on the hot back porch,
rattle our paint cans, point at our clothes
while the old woman squinted up through the screen—
a vague head set on veins hard as coral.
Jolting as if slapped awake, she'd let us in.

Striding by in a sleeveless blouse,
her granddaughter mocked my father's moans
as he papered the walls. She was fat and loud.
When she lifted her arms, I'd glimpse her breasts
and those nipples nosed up like hot little fish

and scorched my insides. One day I breathed deep,
the paint-laden air capsized my sense,
and I took her on the drop-clothed bed.
Dad cursed near the top of the hot high room,
the stepladder popped and squeaked on the walls,

cicadas cheered past the sun-stunned windows
'til she caught me watching, pointed and laughed
as my brush dripped oyster white on my shoes—
cackled as I tried to shake off the trance
and the old woman stuttered up on her cane,

demanded to know who the hell we were.

Love Song for Ray's Exxon and X-rated Arcade

A hot little wind
chirps in the vent
above my dark hot booth
as the soiled screen shimmies
with *Spiked Heels*
The Ecstasy Girls
and the cash register's
scarred yellow bell
sings to the pumps
and they call right back
as I press against
the warped plywood door
fall back into
the cool bright store
where Ray grins big
in his tipped back Stetson
while Lonease and Chainie
schmooze with Wanda
and Ray's new baby
and a woman reading
Housewives in Bondage
says *Hi* says *Have you
heard about Amway?*
and I know that heat
off the prefab Sweet
Union Baptist Church
will stone my eyes
when I leave and I know
we're hopeless
soon gone
good as we get

Love Means Letting Go

That day when we sat knee to knee
        on a mossy river stone
and I braided our fingers together
        and mistakenly kissed my own;

and the night I swept you up in my arms
        and, carrying you to bed,
banged your forehead on the door—
        ah, the things you said;

and that filthy puddle, darling,
        I tried to lift you over
(but who among us has never stepped
        in a manhole that's uncovered?);

and the time I used Vicks Vapo-rub
        when I thought it was KY,
and the way you cursed and leapt about
        and fanned your flaming thighs

are moments I sometimes regret
        when the heart-shaped fall leaves fly,
and make me wonder where you are,
        and with whom, but never why.

Lovington, NM

Though what's to love
is anyone's guess.
Each year more shops
go broke. Each year
the headlights rake
more boarded-up stores
as streets thin out
to frozen dirt roads
where parked teens pump
for crude in the sour
refinery air. Where
hawk-faced wives,
in stalled caravans
of rusting Airstreams,
ask why their men
are pried from their lives
by drill sites and bars,
where tourists, racing
the weather, stop
at Hank's Last Gas
long enough to scrawl
Love, my love, from Lovington
while the postal clerk
cancels each kissed card
and sends them away.

The Pimps Must Be Breaking Arms on Broadway

A hot rain blears the tar.
Two hookers smoke
at a bus stop shelter.

Anchored to the dark,
they rock the white Ls
of their casts.

Only a squad car,
black against streetlights,
slackens their passes.

Soon a man will leave
the finished world
of his sleeping wife.

Blanched by his headlights,
a woman with his
mother's lost look

will stab out a cigarette
on her cast
and walk toward him.

Scene on South Presa

Two kids and a fool
play a kind of game
each day after school.

The man is drunk,
a little lame,
with red eyes sunk

in a swollen face.
It's always the same:
He lunges, they race

off, squeal, circle back,
call him names.
He staggers, hacks,

tries again,
doubles up in pain
as they veer through the gin

on his breath,
dodge the face wet with strain,
arms like death.

Too quick to hold,
the kids tire of the game—
he's just too old—

and they leave him there
as it starts to rain,
empty-handed, kissing air.

My Father Thinks He Lived once Before

Snipped from the *National Geographic*,
photographs arrive by mail inscribed with,
*Prince Edward Island. I remember the hut
made of red stones, the beard that covered my father's
face.*
>*By the way, when you were ten...*
>>>>>>>>>>In a white stucco
>>>>>shack,
he glues together strips of old wood and
sets them in a vise to dry. Folk harps, dulcimers
shine as he hangs them on the walls.
He'll plane down the back of someone's junked spice rack,
>>chisel the fret lines.
>>>>>>Then he's suddenly gone.
Standing on the rock his father pushed off from at dawn,
he stares out to sea.
>>>>>The phone rings.
It's his uncle, a bigwig, owner of the mill,
who talks about margins of profit and loss,
incomes and outgoes 'til my father says,
You want Stinson who? Never heard of the guy,
hangs up and tamps in another fret.
>>>>>>>>>Offshore, a
>>>>>>storm
sends a wind up the bay and it whistles in
the strung nets and red stones.
Tonight they will eat the dried fish by firelight,
take turns making songs to the cod, the tide
and the coming of sons—love songs
to the miracle of what comes back.

Home

Someone must have given up
halfway to the alley.

In backyard weeds
a rocking horse

lies upside-down
on a wadded dress,

a shoebox swollen
with cancelled checks.

Now the rain starts to fall
and the bell in the horse's

broken-out chest
sings to a house

that is silent, cold
and growing dark.

Raymond's Gone Fishing

On the shore of the fields he turns away
from the rutted island, its sheds and machines,
and casts out to the depths of acreage.
The fly fishtails in the dead stands of maize,
the hook drags back with its swipe of dirt.
He angles for the light of his lost brother's watch
that has slowed for years to the turn of furrows.
But nothing's gold on that stalled dusty ocean.
Near the rusted shunt of a John Deere planter,
his wife prays for lightning to stiffen the line,
ground him to the truth and end the matter.
Their quick children circle the banker and sheriff,
scan the air for that nylon arc, keen ears
to the fast affirmation of his spinner.
They think he can reel farms back from nothing,
haul deeds up alive and flashing.
The grit cuts his eyes as he trawls for a stalk
to whip the ground with, witches for a last
trough of rain still inside him.

Homesteading near Lubbock

Once, nothing south of 50th
but windbreak poplars, white square
miles of cotton. Once, nothing
but Grandfather's farmhouse, vacant

now: windmill above the dried up
horse trough charging the air still
with spent minutes, the blackberry
tree where someone's sandals tracked its

bloodied fruit to the porch, past
the screen door drunkenly slung
on one hinge. Inside, there's a
bent syringe on the sill, rusted

bathtub littered with beer caps,
a red sports coat in the stove: teens,
maybe, from sun-spanked suburbs
that, year by year, claim these fields one

house at a time, farm-to-markets
now packed with traffic you can
hear from windows that once brought
only thunder, wind and chickens.

Once, cane chairs schottisched the floorboards,
wheat fields in dust storms roared like surf,
cornered snakes, like sticks with eyes, stood
on their tails and Grandfather sang.

All that's gone. What's left persists

in a new kind of silence.
Outside, newspapers blow in
from work sites, catch on the fence.

They tell how families vanish
overnight, one step ahead
of foreclosure, how someone,
hosing trays of begonias,

has seen something that is both
common and strange: a new house,
open and empty at dawn,
one light left on in the bath.

The Blues

When old Connor died
my grandmother stared
out her kitchen window
at the big blooms waving
in his raked dirt yard, said,
I've got the blues, wiped
her eyes with a dish towel
and went to find work.
She had a right, being
old herself and slow—
or so said the laundry boss
when he fired her. Connor
washed his yard each day,
mended chicken wire
around his prize roses
to keep out the chickens.
Now his house was empty,
open to the weather,
the flowers left to fall,
the hens evicted, wrung
and plucked, but that,
Grandmother would say,
is the way it is all over.
And that's why, now
that I'm older, slower,
I stand in my last brown suit,
unpressed since she died,
and think of Connor—
sovereign of the soak hose,
patriarch of hens and roses—
and get the blues.

Late Summer Comes to Slaton, Texas

1

After a month long strike,
Santa Fe brakemen gun their pickups back to the depot
like hungry farmers heading to a steakhouse.

The older ones grin as they pass *Elaine's Bangs*
where R.T. Bradshaw sits in the service chair
of his late two-timing wife's beauty shop.
His gray crew cut shines in the overhead light
as he thumbs the family album and cries.
   There she is:

showing plenty of leg on the running board
of somebody's roadster
and smiling off.

2

Red lights flicker in municipal leaves.
Back from scraping the remains
of Hank "Young at Heart" McClister
from his semi's sleeper,
the volunteers sip Cokes,
get the checkers out and set up the board.

For days Hank cooked in the hot truck stop lot
'til the cap on his chrome exhaust stack bounced once
and flapped shut.

Now the volunteers' air tanks air out
on the small plot of grass,
bordered by field stones,
under the water tower.

3

At Champion's Jewelry,
J.C. sprawls in a swivel chair,
swipes his face with a big red hanky,
officiates loudly while two Mexicans boys
inch his Mosler safe forward
with a seven-foot pry bar.
The floor tiles pop like pistol fire,
sending up last gasps of bankruptcy dust.

Redistributing his three-hundred pounds
on the straddling casters, J.C shouts,
*Forty year ago you'd a-had a crowd here
to see this happen. Now,* he adds

with a big backhanded wag at the square,
we got this.

4

Jim Butler's rebuilt Triumph
nosily plows lazy eights
on the courthouse lawn.

A rookie pulls up,
slides from his cruiser,
and pulls the rag stopper

from the VFW's "Eternal Flame."
He wipes courthouse grass
off the Triumph's windshield,
takes down the VIN,
takes Jim's keys,
then takes Jim while,
down the darkening streets,
Depression era houses
throw their cats
and little blue squares of TV light
out on the lawns.

Weathering Heaven

1

Bright and dark face off—
burnt orange west and,
to the east,
thunderheads muscling up against night.

In the high, quiet attics,
dust terraced in 2x4 rows
sleeps in the hot stink of newsprint.
Boxed-eared letters and gray, praying clothes
hoard their trunk dark.

Beyond the stilled kitchens,
dust devils waver in the maize.
A rich stroke of lightning Howitzers a yard
and radio voices
spark,
hoarsen with thunder.

Then the deep helmet of the rain.

Wind frets on an abandoned porch.
A chainsaw blade gives back the weather
in bruised, slow passages.

Rain-splats slap vaginal smears
in the dust along post rows.

2

Down cellars we hunker in the onion dark.
No sound.
Then a child's asthma, an overturned car seat.

Then the wide cheer of the dead far off,
the hectoring shrill—
its high-pitched bitching whipping everything.

Sucked out of the lungs,
our breaths stagger out through the door slats,
join all the dead voices that darken the talk
of those swirling arms.

How many rank fucks spice this airloam with salt?
How many limp dishrags of souring marriage
fur the bowels of this storm?

Ants close their earth-pores against it.
Jackrabbits, with a wet shrug,
turn asses windward.
Cattle kneel down, bow into it.

3

The twister whips off, brown and lethal.
The sky unboils,
opens like a childhood.

Held in a rapt moment,
the side-swiped houses list near the gutted cattle.
A black dog cringes in the mud-dashed corner

of a sprung, roofless clapboard.
Waking out of our graves,

we check ourselves for missing parts,
pick gently through the blasted effects.

4.

The sky holds.

All that pour and thrive has mixed the green cut yards
with the scoured fields:
Fists of rusted chain,
lost hunting knives dulled on the meat of seasons,
Comanche points, still sharp, still pointing—
dream-bits from of the land's rich matrix
cast up by the twister's high whine.

5

Whipped by fire truck lights,
we sit on the motherless porches,
stare at the stripped, leaning trees
almost feel the fear and hatred of our deaths
surrender to a grudging desire
to witness it all again:

This sacramental coupling of land and sky.

II. And the animals know we are not at home in our translated world

An Uninvited Guest

It starts with an unsubtle musk,
a low stink that reminds you
of history's ash pits, cul de sacs
where rings of children danced in weeds,
of how they all fell down
with shillings in their armpits.

Something was tumbling
in the wastepaper basket.
A quartet of claws
transected the floor tile
and the house went still, drawn tight
by the penlights of its eyes.

For days it reveled in our bedrooms,
stirred up the sheets
with its impromptu dancing
'til our nightmares bristled
with a whiskery immanence,
with death ships knocking at our docks.

We tamped old magazines
under the doors
to keep it from water,
gassed it with hairspray
when it hid in the closet,
then bought the poison—

cachets of emerald coins
as pretty as candy—
and stashed little caches

of our lovely gift
throughout the house
as if it were Easter.

For days we listened
as the small hands weakened
behind the wainscot, asking
why it didn't belong,
asking why we had sickened it—
our unlovely child

we pitched in the weeds
of a vacant lot
where all things go
to join hands in ashes.

The Charm

Butt first, I'd scoot down the ditch's slick sides
'til my feet touched moss, releasing bubbles
that teased up my legs as I sat half in,
half out of the water. A frog flounced off,
shimmied into a tire, two crayfish danced

together in silt. But all I wanted
were waterdogs mottled with yellow spots
and wreathed in boas of feathery gills.
At my approach, they'd drift from a curtain
of elm roots, rush for the safe black culvert.

One day I slogged out wildly, struck
my knuckles on the stone one hid behind.
Drawing the rock from its suck of mud,
I lunged for its fat slippery middle.
There's a look that stones and salamanders have

when taken indoors. Dour, less wild, they
shift in the counterfeit dark of our rooms.
I filled a tub in the yard with a hose,
dropped the stone on the tub's metal floor
while my mother called and the Chevy idled.

I found it drying to papier-mâché,
waiting on tip-toe when we returned.
Each day I'd squat at the tub's metal rim
and stare at its eyes. Each day those holes
took me deeper in.

Here, Boy!

Our dog skitter-slid
across the kitchen vinyl,
lapping as it drove
its water dish forward.
Is this what those brainy angels saw
when they first touched down
and beamed us aboard?
After all that probing,
did they see at warp speed,
as they chucked us back
to our skullrinds and pinecones,
how their free axe and wheel
would jump-cut to condoms
and cans of New Coke
in our fast-apposing thumbs?
Did they wonder,
as they sailed away
to new assignations—
their DNA helixing
through our veins—
which of us would be first
to slip like Rex
and hit the fridge?

The Chimps at Hendler's Welding

I'd rub a black hole in the glass door's gleam,
peer through the jungle of cable and scrap
where they thrashed about in makeshift cages.
Midnights, I'd often stop there and wonder
what ape god sentenced them to the deafening
slam-dance of steel and blinding acetylene.
I needed to pity these little men
with the flailing arms and frantic glances—
glances returned when I dropped off orders
from Trammell Printing. On the graveyard shift,
I'd wash the platens with leaded gas,
curse, with my bucket of pliers and rags,
under the quaking guts of the presses.
The owner's chain-smoking, hard-drinking widow
had jammed my cot between two steel cabinets
and nailed a print to the opposite wall.
In it, three dogs, wearing bow ties and bowlers,
puffed at fat cigars and played poker.
I'd flop on the cot in my ink-thumbed apron
and stare at this trio. Poker-faced,
they regarded their hands with a simple,
heart-breaking incomprehension.
It was funny and it wasn't and I'd laugh,
howl and rattle my cabinets.

Cow in the Suburbs

At midnight a Holstein,
wakened far from the herd,
calls and calls as the echoes bounce
off the condos and rentals across from the range land.

When she hears my shoes clatter out on the asphalt
she trots to the fence,
stands in her half of our circle of streetlight
and stares,
then gallops back to the dark
and bellows again.

I pull handfuls of grass,
stand in the surf of trash at the fence line
crying, *Ho boss Ho boss*
'til she steps closer,
stops,
lifts a foreleg.

But I'm still not a cow
and she turns,
bounds farther out to her world
of twisted mesquite and starlight.

All I can see is her white throat
as she mourns and mourns for her lost family.
I throw down the grass,
thumb the rusted barbed wire.

When I was six I led our milk cow home with a rope.
It got dark. I was scared.

The cow felt like a mountain beside me.
First the road disappeared, then the hills
and I whimpered as I stumbled through the loose gravel.
Then the slack rope tightened and she brought *me* home.

I can still feel that massive and generous ease
striding beside me.
Then this lost granddaughter startles me back—
her hoarse calls echoing in
the patios and brick barbecue pits
of Chateau Eight and Helves Lane.

Listening to Cattle in the City

At first you think of meadows
when you hear them lowing,
fields of grass where some rustic chap
is plowing or mowing.

Then suddenly the bales of hay
change to buildings
with sliding hooks, trenches in floors
that are filling and flowing.

Quickly the calls turn to cries,
though it's still a steady lowing—
a dirty trick played by the heart
to trouble our ears with knowing.

Age

At dawn,
with nothing to do, I went down
to a closed sidewalk café
just coming to life with the sound
of waiters banging plates,
then took a street to the river.
The sun was nudging up
and casting mounds of silver
on the cold slow-moving water

when sudden crowds
of pigeons bustled down
from the undersides of bridges,
heading for their jobs in town,
the parks and high-rise ledges.
Then a sharper, quicker noise:
bats taking back their hide-outs
after a night with the boys.
And suffering all this joy,

sat an old pigeon who frowned,
with one red eye fixed to the ground
while those leather-jacketed thugs
yawned and hung around.
Age—I understood!—
comes to everything, even *that*.
I watched it keep its shit-stained place,
fractious,
attended by bats.

Loneliness at Fort Clark

> Kiss cats: for the deer and the dachshund
> are one.
> —Wallace Stevens

The gentrified barracks bask
in the confident Fort Clark sun.
A CPA in paisley shorts
interrupts his morning run
to shoo three deer off his lawn.
Lagging behind, a fawn

gets cornered, caught and sprayed
for ticks by a Miss Raposa,
who wavers back to the shade
to nip at her mimosa.
The circumspect Fort Clark sun
nods to just about everyone

but me. I sulk past while my ex—
or rather, soon to be—
takes coffee on the verandah
and ever so quietly
discusses me with her parents.
Out of work, out of place, *errant*,

I stray near the foot of a hill
where the bulkhead of an arsenal
bleeds rust still
on the golf course footpath,
then loiter onto the links
while the bushed Fort Clark sun sinks.

By the sick klieg light of the moon,
a broker strolls out to the pool
to show the sky to his cat—
waves its paw for it, the fool.
Now the deer and the dachshund are one.
Sun down and out, dead and gone,

I'll hunt this cellblock town.
Like the bats, I'll soar
and bite things out of the air
as I make my nightly run
past row on sequestered row
of these garrisoned citizens—

but that's not for everyone.

Stepping into a Peepshow at the End of 1977, I Think of Rilke's *Tenth Elegy*

> "And just in back of all this: the real, children at play,
> lovers embracing and, off to one side, dogs at the serious
> bidding of nature in thinning grass."

Slam-bang out of the blaze of day,
I grope to an ill-lit stall where
lust performs to the perturbations

of worn-out reels. Crav-
ing to come, I've found this bazaar
of nonstop fornication

where age-
less skin flickers in an Otherwhere
beyond extinction.

If the lens strays
first here, then there
for no particular reason,

if the aging tint fades
and the shaved cheerleader's hairs
fall green, then gold, miming our seasons,

if the unchapped cowboy gyrates
through endless yards of rickety film in bare-
backed coition,

just say
it's our fault. These are
deathless despite our shaky perceptions.

What they betray
is capitalized US: sex fairs
where genitals, on display for promotion,

shine like cash and everyone pays
or sells in the klieg light glare
of trickle down consumption.

Angels of entrepreneurial lust, they
take what would sour
our flaccid hearts past putrefaction...

Spread on '70s shag, a lubed brunette waves
to the camera, waves at me here
in a booth rank with masturbation.

O sprocketed light! Play
on, play out, play everywhere,
as befits such gods of bi-location.

I stumble away
with the after-burn of that soundless glare.
The wind and sun's redemption

washes me back to my life where
our kids make out for free and the neighbor-
hood dogs don't just go through the motions.

III: Where smoke goes

Ballad of the Cotton Compress

It was a grim cathedral
of steam and rusty tin.
Each quick vent from its stack would call
more loads from the smoking gins.

Flat trucks came in the nighttime,
flat trucks came all day,
and lint-furred men, both young and old,
bore the brick-tight bales away.

My grandmother stood at the window
of Slaton Dry-cleaning and Steam,
brought down the press on a cotton dress
and straightened another seam.

My grandmother stared through the window
at the brick hospital's third floor,
said, *Today a little bale will be dropped
on the porch of the world's front door.*

The street sharpened out to blacktop,
to picked-clean fields under ice.
My grandmother rubbed her knees, thought
how it hadn't been so nice

to crawl down long hot furrows
and fill a long limp sack
'til it deadened with dirty cotton
for a few coins dropped in her lap.

She'd pack her gums with cotton

plucked from an unripe bole
and let the good ache numb the hours
as night came on, and the cold.

Gray fans in the laundry
turned in the red brick walls.
Gray lint fell from the metal blades
and drifted into balls.

My uncles were drunk on the railroad,
my aunts were buying TVs,
my father was shacked at the Lone Star Inn
with the girl from the corner café.

Grandmother felt her life loosen
and slip to the concrete floor
like a cotton sack's sweat-stained strap
when it's not any good anymore.

Snow in the hospital window
tumbled down like lint.
The reverend read from a little white book:
You're wretched, he said. *Repent.*

The doctor stood over my mother
and turned my wet swirled head—
mid-century, a month past Christmas.
It's time. Press down, he said.

Called Out

While my cold toes motioned
under the blanket
he'd arrive with the noise
of breaking trains—
clock face glazed
by rain and the screen
while night whistles called
all the fathers away,
their swung lamps
scooping horizon light.

Smoke from his mouth
snaked through the screen,
played through my small hands
as his eyes flared up
and out like signs.
The homes broke free
like lovesick bells,
took the engine yard's
iron wheels and left,
trailing their skirts

down the bricked streets.
By dawn he was gone,
the houses back on their lots,
but scarred.
I was picked from the crib,
rolled out to cold light
by a host of hands
to see the rubbed-out
butts on the sill.

When Lewis Punched the Valdez Kid—

I climbed
to the local height
of a neighborhood shed,
strapped on my Junior Hohner accordion
and flailed away at "Home Sweet Home."

Dan clanged up on his polio braces,
offered to kick my ten-year-old ass
and we wrestled on the hot tarred tin
while city pickups revved their foggers
and drowned our houses in DDT.

Then they came—a blitzkrieg
of BB guns, branches, bricks and boards pouring
out of the smoking dog pens and shacks,
past the schoolhouse simmering like an arsenal—
flattening everything in its path,
hot to get Lewis.

We heard him go down
with a small, surprised cry
and it was over.

Danny clanked home in his armor
while the killers fell back and milled around.
I snatched up my squeezebox,
whimpered and wheezed—
its reedy breath wafting up from my lap,
that corny tune flapping
like taffy in my hands.

Range-testing

Blue as the heavens it plunged from,
freckled with rust where it nosed into
the flat-packed dirt and wind-sheared grass
spreading up to the test grounds, the test grounds
graying out in haze. Jerry patted the base,

then gripped its tapered, two-foot length
and brought it forth while the Texas sky
stood still and two rabbits watched from a hill.
Alive with silence, lit by the glossy
wrinkled spines of Mickey Spillane,

it stood in Jer's room. I said, *Your niece
will break in here and blow us to hell*
as Lisa banged in, flashed her crotch
and raced out. At the caliche pit,
our pocketknives worked faster at

the soft white clay. The pristine slugs
were pocketed, prized, the blunted ones
tossed in the road that ran through the pit—
the road where Mrs Glish and the coach
got caught in the back of her husband's blue Dodge.

Jack Glish drove the school bus. Scrawny bald cowboy
in discount boots and sprayed-on jeans,
he'd sneak quick hits from a paper bag,
swing wide and bank the back tires off
the shouldered curves. Near the end of the run

we'd light cheap cigars and let the blue smoke trail
up the Trammell girl's nose. We were men.
We were moving. We didn't care.

At the Food Bank

Are we supposed to eat this stuff?
A can falls spewing to the floor.
Her words, one by one, erupt.

She bends to pick her toddler up.
Everyone can see she's poor.
Are WE supposed to eat this stuff?

She asks again. *I've had enough.*
Her throat is bruised, her eyes, sore.
The can spins on the floor, erupts.

Someone comes with pail and mop,
Someone leaves to get her more.
Yes, you're supposed to eat this stuff,

Someone says, officious, gruff.
A sick off-white, the spoiled soup pours
Along a wall. Two words erupt

From a tight, lined mouth: *Life's tough.*
Somewhere someone slams a door.
She takes a box crammed with the stuff.
Hate feeds on hunger, erupts.

Ballad of Mackenzie Park

Located in Lubbock, Texas, this municipal park bears the name of Col. Ranald Slidell (Bad Hand) Mackenzie of the U.S. Cavalry. Under his command, the Southern Column massacred 1,400 Indian ponies near Palo Duro Canyon on 28 September 1874, forcing the Kiowa and Cheyenne to begin the long march back to the agencies of that year. Diagnosed as suffering from "paralysis of the brain" in 1883, Mackenzie died three years later.

> O master, who are those
> Whom the tempestuous blackness castigates?
> —Dante's *Inferno*

The park spread in the moonlight,
a graveyard stripped of stones.
I drove in through the red brick gate
so we could be alone

and followed one of three dim roads
up one of three low hills
that overlooked the wind-smeared lake.
Jane was edgy, ill.

I backed into the shadows
cast by two tall trees,
set the brake, looked at Jane,
nervously shook my keys.

Jane slowly took her clothes off.
We climbed into the back.
She rubbed her cigarette out, exhaled,
groaned, then mounted my lap.

Later, we sat and listened
as the first cold front of the year
spat and hissed in the heater vents
and the windshield shed its tears.

A slum sprawled up to the railroad
behind Mackenzie Park.
Distant junk fires faltered, flared
in the storm surge and the dark.

Nearing, the junk smoke tumbled
over the Santa Fe rails,
scudded south across the lake
and died in the wind's cold wail.

Jane suddenly threw my coat on
and started for the lake.
I knew what was going to happen,
knew that an old hard ache

would seize her if we came here
and send her out to stalk
the place where she had suffered.
Now she began to talk.

Miseries poured from her
as I followed in the dark,
tired litanies of sorrow
dredged up by Mackenzie Park:

She was married and forty,
I was twenty and not.
Next to my shame and failure,

what, she said, *have* you *got?*

Words hurled over her shoulder
were heavy with middle-aged ills:
death, divorce, estrangement.
I'd be crushed by her wheels.

I kicked at the wind-burnt clover
and lamely said I loved her.
She crossed her thin arms tighter
and started walking faster.

We halted by the lake.
Why do I come here? she said.
I tried to answer, stammered,
saw where she pointed her hand.

A swan lay in the rushes,
killed with a bottle of beer.
Its neck lay in the water,
one white wing on a tire.

She hurried off. I followed.
The park lights smeared her hair.
She muttered, hugged her shoulders.
I knew we were almost there.

I caught her, tried to hold her.
She cursed, broke free, rushed on.
I shouted, *Let's go to Jim's Donuts*.
She looked back once and was gone.

Long ago, her son had pedaled

down the lane where the park ran south,
had placed his books on a fresh-cut stump
and a handgun in his mouth.

I knew she had gone the next morning
to kneel where he'd been found,
had pulled up fists of tough, thick grass
'til her nails raked the dark oily ground.

It had been a bright winter morning.
Two policemen, standing near
had chatted about something amusing,
but quietly, so she wouldn't hear...

Now, sleepwalking in a nightmare,
Jane stopped where the lane ran south,
stood and stared at the rotting stump
where her son put the gun in his mouth.

Blanched by an oval of park light,
the grass, like scum on the lake,
said nothing of what had happened.
All that was left was the ache

that drove her here each winter
to park on the same low hill
and stare past the same wind-smeared lake
while dash vents hissed in the chill.

Now I am forty years older
and go to Jim's Donuts alone.
I stare through the plate glass window
at that graveyard stripped of stones

and think about Jane and her son
as the first winter storm rushes in,
sending junk smoke scudding across the lake
to the place where the stump had been.

On Not Painting Vacant Farmhouses in Sulphur Bluff, Texas

You will find them at the ends of unmown roads
among fallen sheds,
dusty clumps of ragged elms. No

two are alike, although the entropy
that haunts each of them
makes them seem half dream, half memory.

Wadded carpets sprawl at the gate
where the slugged-in rural box exclaims
ANTON SCHERTZ in red barn paint.

The doors are nailed, swollen closed by rain,
so I shimmy backwards
under a sash, dive into a wreck

where broken bottles crunch like coral
and window light plays
on the aging wallpaper's tea-dark floral.

The warped floorboards cry out with each footstep,
then stiffen against me.
Touched, the painted glass doorknobs flake

like a child's nail polish. But this house
is childless, so possessed
by its fine cold mold that I'm turned back out

into windy sunlight to lie in the jimson.
One eye half open,

I watch two buzzards regard the crimson

flecks on my work clothes. But, dead as I seem
as they vacillate,
not one drops close to let me know those wings

and eyes. Only Wade lives close enough to watch.
Bald from chemo,
he smokes on his porch and tries to keep down lunch.

I toss a horse apple to Wade's old roan. At the sound,
he moseys over
and noses the treat to lonelier ground

while Wade, like his smoke—that pale and thin—
tries to rise,
settles back and lights up again.

# VI. Roads and rivers

Halloween on the Serengeti

I saw teeth and clawed walls—
that lethal grin—
as he worked at wrecking the botched kitchen counter.

Outside, she sat in the dark and downpour,
wiped her eyes
with lipstick-smeared forearms.

But her feints and flights and silences
couldn't save us.

Sis and I were just kids.
All we could do was hide out
while his legs switched by like knives,

watch the trick or treaters scatter
as he ruined the kitchen
with saws and supper.

Washed-out stores poured
their goods down the streets:
plastic skulls, white shocks of hair

on wizened masks, ghost sheets rolling
up on the lawn,
lolling back in the wash

like thawed winter kills...
I still can see him:
Sawdust on his mouth,

he comes out and rests against her
like a jackal weary from the kill—
the four of us staring off

while the street drags away
its pelts and bones.

Charlie Parker

Not the musician, but an old black man
who owned half a block of shotgun shacks
hammered up one summer in '41.

I painted houses and liked the ghetto,
with its ink-slick ditches, chained dogs,
chicken wire threading with mint-green vines

and the dusty dead-end street named Sadie
where Charlie's six kids rested their chins
on the cool sills of the back alley windows.

Cane crooked around his bony neck,
he sat straight-backed as his '46 Ford
jarred us to the store for more paint.

Trouble is, peoples don leans to the church,
was all he said to the clerk who refused
his preacher credit. And when a fat man

huffed across Main in a three-piece suit,
Charlie laughed and said, *The banker's failin.*
Hornets nested in the eaves of his houses.

If he heard me curse and swat my ball cap,
he'd spit tobacco juice on his palm
and thumb down the sting 'til it cooled.

While evening stretched its shadows to the curb,
he'd shout, *Fred Steel, turn the wheel*
as a neighbor's Chevy smoked up the drive.

I thought of West Crosby—called Silk Stocking Lane—
on the white side of town. No one sang
anyone home when I worked *that* street.

Inspiration Hills 90

Up-gathered at dawn
by this too hot, over-lit
twelve-ton lozenge hauling
hell bent down
a congested Styx of red exhaust,
we are the damned poor.
Our Mexican driver's mustache rides
a river littered with *shits* and *fucks*
worn smooth with use.
Heads loll with lane changes,
hypnotized by the killing sense
they deserve nothing better—
and we *are* no better
than the fast food trash back-
sliding down the aisle.
In paint-stained Goodwill
and broken dress shoes,
I'm poorer than most.
My finger tips,
when I grip the seatback,
burn with malnutrition.
A fry cook lays his 90-proof breath
flat against my neck.
A nurse glares past us—
beehive teased to a lacquered fight
above cracked pancake makeup.
Only the mad, who grieve
from the witness boxes of their seats,
are along for the ride.

Behind us stand the flimsy doors
of our shitty rentals where
rats snuff the joists, steal out
and eat the bath soap by roachlight.

The interior richens
with greasy sacks
and plundered lunch pails.
My faints come and go—
empty rooms I pass through smoothly.
The vomit breath of a mission kitchen
wafts out of an alley
as the bus downshifts
past a slurring filmstrip
of sullen storefronts,
trailing police tape
and bleeding neon,
then stops.

Like wide-eyed fish hauled
dead from the depths,
we sprawl down and out
to the bat-loud pallor
of a wage slave morning—
some of us clutching transfers.

LeOta Hodge Talks About Life

I can't have all that goin away
come back on me—not with Wayne gone
and the twins in Quitman. You come around
with those fishsticks and that orangeade
like the King of Sheba, but in a week
you'll turn and go as bad as that fish.
Not that I'd care. Not that I'm any good
for much anymore. Just look at them legs.
In high school I had knees like Betty Grable,
then sliced them up on a trashcan lid
tryin to outrun Tal. Scars? Can't show you
if I don't know you. But don't pucker up.
I got a few good licks in, too.
Aunt Bess used to cry that Uncle Jess took
my shinkicks to his grave. Like he didn't need them.
Like him and the rest didn't earn those kicks
in the chicken coop behind the barn.
But damn, if they didn't all get me back
when I tangled my legs in the steerin wheel
of Daddy's new Dodge. Them spankin the bumpers,
hootin like a pack of horny owls
while I fought to get my dress to my knees.
Now it's just me and this exercise bike
that Wayne made out of Chainie's junked Schwinn.
If I don't pump this thing morning and night
my legs twitch and ache so much I can't sleep.
Doc Sween says my legs are all in my head.
If he says that again these legs will give him
a piece of their mind. Lord, what I'd give
to not sleep in fits and wake up pumpin
this one-wheel wonder up to Wayne in heaven.

Tired as I am, you could burn down all the
beds in Texas. Keep your Kool-Aid and fish.
You men grab the wishbones of our legs.
Either way we break, you get your wish.

Nepo Road

(Carrizo Springs, 1984)

Here, sidewalk-sized,
there, wide as a car,
its asphalt stretched
through range land mesquite.

Slogging through the heat
to class, I'd catch
two deer leaping tar
to the other side.

Tails up, they'd glide
past tire
tracks cross-hatched
with prints of bare feet.

Here, where my students met
to spark and catch
fire
in the best lover's lane this side

of that south Texas town, I thought of lost nights
when, hot-wired,
a girl and I clutched
in a Ford parked in West Texas wheat

and wore-out the backseat.
Inexhaustible lust?
Just thinking about it makes me tired,
but reminds me how, in time,

all that abides
of passion, after the sour
sanctions of church
and state,

will be, soon and late,
a soft ditch,
stiff tissues in the weeds, our
notes the rain opens to *Jill loves Ryan*.

Let's Go

He remembered the tow of his mother's voice,
how she led him through fields where heads of maize
whipped him like blades: *Jay, wipe your face
 and let's go.*

Now he sat in the squad car, sweated and twitched
as the cop grazed through the stained, misfolded maps
in his car.

His seized handgun shone in the dash lights,
the handcuffs made it a kind of game:
How quick would he be as the rookie strode back,
the vial of heroin tumbling
in his palm?

The gun was helplessly light with his luck
as the muzzle flash struck the patrolman's head.
Jay fell miles, awoke in a vacant garage
to voices, a fist on the peeled metal door,
to one hard dream grinding into
another.

When they baptized him in a converted boiler,
when he stumbled out, embraced the first man,
and walked back to his cell on death row
he was soaked, joyous, scared as hell and
almost home.

Fjords

Squaring his back
against a chipped green wall,
he banked two bolts
off a chipped green door,
said, *Cut yourself.*
Bleed out of here.
I've been here before.
Six weeks in the hole.
On a stinking cot,
I said Fjord fjord
til those cold arms roped
my wrists and towed me
over mountains, fields
and I woke clean-shaved
in a room scrubbed by sunshine.
Hide a blade for light
and remember the fjords,
he said and stretched
a scarred wrist for his dice.

National Corpse

Televised, even a small excavation southwest of Verdun
brings quick rewards: shrapnel, spent slugs, one
corpse, then three, pushed, no doubt, before they could rot,
into a shell hole downwind of a trench
that's now a faint scar in farmland—one inch
if, while passing by plane, you measured by thumb.
Thousands, ninety years ago, died in this mud.
Now a co-ed, over from Hull and helping out,
gently trowels clay from a bone-filled boot
while her prof., on loan to the BBC,
checks his tie in a rearview mirror and speaks
in a calm, authoritative tone
about snipers, salients, mortar concussion—
all of the nasty business of dying for the state.
But the big and obvious question remains:
How did a bunch of interrelated royals
churn this earth into a boiling barb-wired mass
of blasted trees, blown-off faces
face-up on the roads—all hung with the unshake-
able stink of cordite, alcohol-soaked bandages,
dead horses, dead men?
The docent finds a button.
So much for individual human loss
when she wipes it clean, finds that it's embossed
with flames and declares it French.
She peers down a buried line that dimples
Belgian fields, waits a full eight seconds,
then tells the boom mike, *First and last,*
these bones will be handled with respect
'til proper burial. But I get
a different take: These serve again as extras

while the couched and snacking masses
fondle remotes and watch
the dead, resurrected piecemeal, drift off
like smoke, or closing credits, or banished thoughts.

Making 84

They had names like Eddy, Steve and Bill.
One summer they broke
the old highway up
a chunk at a time
all the way to Lubbock.

Standing on a chair
at my grandmother's window,
I'd watch them winch a big pig iron ball
'til it hung
motionless in the wind. Then

down it would come like thunder,
the fat chain slackening.
Men home from the war—
their shirtless backs whelped by rifle fire
in places called Burma and Mindanao—

they'd heave those unwieldy
chunks on the truck,
smile back through cigarette smoke and sweat
at the new lanes nearing
in a haze of hot tar.

These men had children who rode those backs
when they drove home at dusk,
young wives who salved
zigzags of proud flesh
as they leaned into their new TVs.

I grew up watching them grow old,
watched their once quick grins
soften and fall
as their bow ties floated
close to my nose,

in clouds of talc at Lemmon's Barbers,
watched their fast hands falter
sacking groceries at Haddock's.
Far from the shellfire and thunder,
those scarred backs rest on satin.

I take the roads they helped lay down
so long ago, touch
their crossed hands—veins
like stopped lightning,
stiff as candlewick.

Agent Orange

The playa lake behind Henzler's pig farm
smelled like the pigs. When it spilled into
a nearby gorge to Yellow House Canyon,
we took that stony staircase down, whoop-jumped
through a muddy flood to the canyon floor's
serene green and birdcall.
                              Now a bone disease
has thinned you to this: Hair cropped short, face
x-rayed to ash, you punch my house with a crutch
strapped to your three-wheel bike, stab at my life
of notepad and book 'til I open the door.
Twirling a bolt on your steel-braced leg,
you dip into a pouch of Red Man chew,
lean down, spit and tell a joke so cruel
I want to give you that flood, that floor.

M.I.A.

The transistor radio tingling my cheek,
I'd climb our hill in Fabe Stahl's meadow.
From that house-high giant's grave of stones
I'd watch three cows seem to drink the earth,
peck rabbits off with my arm and wonder
if you hunted in a darker world than the one
greening around me. When I shook the radio,
brush fires of voices sizzled with Asia.
In your heavy tan jacket, I'd ask Orion,
Is he pinned down? Is he nearing daylight?
But the whiff of a dead calf came with rain,
the stones just shrugged and muttered beneath me.
Now, when my thumb roams the air for your wavelength
your curses shuttle across the stations
and bleed back to space. I shoulder the ghost
of your M-16, say *Over and out*
to the speaker's deaf white oval and
wade down through the waist-high grass
as the distant porch lights signal me in.

Highway E90

Gather them up
on the road from Al Basra
to Takrit. Pick up Valdez,
get Cade and Malone,
find Klattenhoff's tags
and his heavy boots.
Then gather the men
who lay by the road:
Tariq's hands, the legs
of Wahab. And Rawa,
the girl who lived by the road,
please take her, too,
and the empty dress.
These pieces are made
in your image. Lord,
gather them up.

Uirsche's First Three Decades

1

The years stride away and Uirsche, aged ten,
stands sentry again on the side-stepped strip of old 84
   in his native Jerome.

Uirsche paces as the big-faced moon
blushes up orange from the black flat fields,
blanches to cold anger and arcs off to the west.

He sorrows as the Santa Fe coaches,
lit with bright plates, blonde hair and silver,
   slide past glum Jerome.

2

The years do a shuffle through Elmira, Texas—
years so sharp his palms ached in the butane dark
   of his step-father's Airstream.
Naked and thin on a cot, he dreams of tall women
while range land wavers under miles of sunlight.
August from Elmira to Maljamar
seeps deep into his eighteen-year-old bones
as the women stride off, their high breasts
   beyond him.

With quarts of Schlitz stowed under the dash
   of his '65 Olds,
he stomps the gas from Elmira to Lubbock,
pounds the horn past his father's dark house
   as the radio yells

Never can say goodbye, drones the endless war.
The stars pitch and swoon in the hood of his car

    all the way back to Elmira.

3

Last night, thunderheads rumbled up from the Gulf,
snapped the necks of the elms next door,
struck down the grackles and sparrows as they slept.

Now his three-year-old wobbles among the stunned fists of
        fluff and pats each chick.
Tonight, when lightning cuts her toy-strew floor into
        cold little moments,
he'll remember the scarred helmet from his father's war,
how he curled in a ditch and bit his knees as the German
        .88s fell on Arnhem.

Beyond his help, in a rail yard near Poznan, his father
        half-slept
with his head propped against a cattle car's scarred dark
        withers,
slept upright against a child who scratched

13 Juli 41
Ich bin Lya Graf

on her arm with a thumbnail.

Who can we save?
The long freights are unloaded at night.

Lake Watauga Drawdown

> In memory of Old Butler, Tennessee

First, water crawled up to City Hall,
then fattened far back
of the schoolhouse,
filling the church's freshly vacated graves.

The drugstore parking lot sank, the pool
at the Y went down
as a lake, like night,
rose, drowning the town. For years, children,

crossing in boats, felt fishing lines catch
in family trees,
or snag the flagpole.
Daydreaming above the streets' silted grid

or rowing in sleep, they saw kin, still young,
float up from home,
then turn back to
the water's dark arctic. Hauled up on a post,

a rain gauge was an inch below normal.
Weathercocks
traded wind
for the spillway's direction while roped tires

swayed from drowned elms and windmills turned, bringing
water to water.
Then lightning rods started witching for rain

and the heights of children on long lost doorframes
became indelible.
Now the Water Board
opens one flood gate and closes another.

Surrounded by the undersound
of retreating water,
the children come back
to touch remembered streets with their canes.

All the dark arms are letting them go
as they sit on porches,
talk past dawn and
try to wipe all the light from their eyes.

ized %. And then night was there

Everyone Needs a Job. Everyone Needs to Be in Touch

Take Hettie Netlinger,
90 years young,
who lives at the bend
of County Road 40.
People stop there often.
The road runs straight for miles and miles,
cars sail past the place where the Slow sign was stolen and WHAM,
dead-end into Hettie's old oak.
Tonight it's Hightower,
first name: Connie,
late of Konnie's Kurios.
Aroused by the crash,
Hettie swings out of bed
like a girl of 60,
grabs her broom and goes sweeping
out of the house, sweeps
across her dirt yard, stops
and pockets a ceramic gnome.
At the ruptured van,
she backhands Connie
off the steering column,
pats the dead eyes shut
as a few loosened leaves
slide idly down
the spavined windshield.
Pivoting nimbly,
she sweeps back to her house,
its glum untouched clutter,
and tosses the gnome

with the broken watch,
bloodied veil and box of teeth,
then leaps back to bed
as the digital clock's
little red bones
say it's never too late.

Hot Day at Hank's Wrecks and Derelict Drive-in

Lug nut mobiles, hot hubcap medallions
danglebang
on the Coke signs bolted to rain-stained stucco

at Hank's concession stand-turned-office.
And yes, the main
attraction is Hank's sense of humor:

He's aimed the nose of each scorched Pinto,
each blown Nissan
and totaled DeVille at the drive-in screen.

Wrecks cook in the grid of weedy dirt roads,
seem to listen
with their broken or rolled down windows

for the ghost buzz in the headless speaker posts'
twin cut wires.
Oil taps at the heart of each chassis's shadow,

bald tires softly whisper themselves flat as,
sick of the wince
and ache of miles, the carbodies await resurrection

on the disassembly line of the dead.
Their memories
of the world beyond the high tin fence

are fading to sun-baked
upholstery

as they squat amid stacked Brancusi-esque bumpers

and squiggling contentions of heater hoses
under the arch
de triomphe of wheel rims for Henry Frizzell—

smelling of Schlitz, the gas leak du jour
and cheap cigars—
to come cut them down until nothing's left

but rows of hoods propped up like stone sails
whose shadows reach
for the blank screen at the speed of night.

House in the Country

A small boy yelps in the cold until he's tired,
stares up at the room where his mother was found.
A dead crow dangles from a tree in the yard.

Beneath his boots, the walnut shells are hard.
He sets his foot, awaits the sound,
then yelps to shake the knowledge he is tired.

The house is filled with cans of rancid lard,
unopened mail, old work clothes, mildewed gowns—
all dead as the crow that dangles in the yard.

Back from work, exhausted, soured
by wheat field sweat, the father pounds
the windshield, beckons to his child, who's tired

of the trash which, day by day, grows higher.
He yelps at his father, shapes a mound
of broken shells and stomps it in the yard.

Light from the late sun falls in shards
from his mother's window to the ground—
the window where she'd said, *I'm tired*
to the crow that called and called in the yard.

Brief Museums

For Kay

Your wind chimes still sing together on the porch.
Ralph, your black lab, rank with fall rain,
mopes under a lawn chair.
Next week he'll be sold.

But you, in powder-blue scrubs,
sweat matting your blond-gray bangs
as you vacuumed the den to TV music,
are an emblem of how we have, then suddenly
haven't, the world.

Trim and little at 53,
you practiced a circumspect civility
as I came and left by the backroom stairs.
Each morning, your garage door woke me up
as it rattled under my apartment floor.
Each evening, it woke me up again
as you came home laden with night school books.

When the vein behind your pale bangs burst,
you fell to the kitchen's black and white vinyl.
Now your house is quiet,
a brief museum of sudden ends:
the lipstick on your last kissed Kleenex,
Ernest Becker's *The Denial of Death*
face down on the thread box.

And it's true: These displays,
which will soon be boxed, tossed out, forgotten,

deny you have died, seem to wait for you
to come back humming
and spill your books on the dining room table.

Emptied of you,
this house will reopen to other lives,
and that battered garage door,
which has suffered so many comings and goings,
will tremble up like an old trustee
and let them in.

Watching the Mad Sleep

Lights out
at the Granville Home for Men.

Vince turns in a surf
of bent cigarettes.

Jay plunges under
hugging fistfuls of ball caps.

The rest just list like
poor in steerage

or wrecks taking water.
The red exit sign

beams a last word of warmth
as the thermostats wring

cold from the cold
and seize.

Nightshift trustee,
I check locks, count meds

while the house tries to shake
the air conditioner's grip on the roof.

In a vacant closet,
a cardboard carousel

teeters on a greasy shelf.

Flicked forward,
dusty licorice bats and stale sugar ghosts
tremble a little

from odd bits of string.
Then the wheel grinds back

on its axle,
stops.

The Wall Clock at Miss Edna's Boardinghouse

Cut from plywood in her brother's shop,
mounted to the works of an aging West Bend,
its wide face stared as the hour hand, fixed
to a popsicle stick, edged her dying father
toward his next pill. Propped with old books
in the old four-poster, he'd sputter and wheeze
as she pressed a paper cup to his mouth
and sponged his chest as the pain did its work.
Edna's brother was a taxidermist.
One day I was stopped by a bobcat drying
on the kitchen table. Snarl set with pins,
it faced a fan as the little bursts
thumbed its fur. The morning I left,
I watched the numerals, scrawled in nail polish,
harden out of the dark, the cup dispenser's
cold gleam lengthen on the opposite wall.
Did the old man pray? Were there times he couldn't?
I waited as the hand touched six, shuddered, healed,
and marched toward nightfall.

Cauthorn

In a white wicker chair
painted so many times
it looks like stone,
she sits,
the mottled sticks
of her hands like bone,
nothing but time
on those hands. She cares

for nothing, stares
as the white lines
of kin blur past, wants to go home.
Finger tips
of wind pick
at the hem of her housecoat. She groans,
spanks her hearing aid, whines
that the cat will tear

the curtains if she's not there,
remembers it's dead, says *Nevermind*,
asks for an ice cream cone.
She looks straight at me, says *Sit*.
*I almost had a chicken fit
when I saw you. This house yours? You know,
I played in the basement back in '05.
It still there?*

*I even dared
ride on Von Hein's
slick black coffins. You didn't know
this place was a funeral home, I bet.*

*I'd put
my brother's straw boater on, roam
the canebrakes, sight
redskins hiding under bear*

*robes or, putting on airs,
to hounds we would ride.
Help me up. Let's go.
I want to sit
on one of those black caskets a bit.
You can pack me in satin and foam
tomorrow. Today I want a ride.
Take me there.*

My Kid Sister and the X-ray Machine

This woman I once
taught to eat mud,
buttons her lab coat,
steps behind a lead-draped wall,
and sees straight through me.

That her gestures are so
practiced, professional—
all good-natured sisterly revenge
now left outside the chiropractor's door—
is unnerving. Again,

the dead clunk and low hum
as the lethal light burns
my skeleton's ghost
into the black slick film.
And there they are:

enlarged prostate,
arthritic spur, skull
slightly tilted left.
Left! The sinister side—
death's direction.

My sister's round face
arches, sharpens.
I wish somebody would laugh,
poke my ribs, slap my back
as she hands me the dark

little pool of my clothes.

Failing Heaven

The red doors met.
Out the gasketted windows
my life streaked away
with an easy swish
I wished my heart had.

Tethered to my drips, I raced
face-up through floors,
my soul a rope trick
going *and and*
while a helicopter,

like a skeletal angel,
vacillated past
the plate glass windows.
The oxygen clip's little blizzard
whizzing up my nose,

I watched kinfolk blow
through Intensive Care
like search parties bent
by winds of worry
to hover above

each foreclosed face.
The cath lab looked
like a metal motel room.
Here, what begins
with a slit in the groin,

ends at the heart's roadblock
dyed red with warning.
Caught in the monitor's
iced-over smile,
my bloody little squatter

banged in its hammock
of greasy strings.
Frowning down,
God's big demolitionist's face
slapped my ribbed shack back

to its casters intact.

Burying My Book

Off I-35,
rest stop sleep
gave me back the road,
and the center line,
flicking beneath my lids,
dragged me back and I passed
the whisky-soaked
bonfires of home, passed
the rusted-shut dustbin
of each failed school.
The women I'd known
were refugees fleeing
a smoking town,
the schools where I worked,
burning my secret
to ashes with talk,
were locker-lined alleys
storming with trash,
with the greasy, wadded
maps of my life.
My car rear-ended
an immigrant farm.
Fishing my book from the air,
I curled it into a jar.
Deep-stepping out
to the pit of a field,
I clawed past the matrix
of rotted stalks, soft
splinters of long gone
dolphin-shaped hames,
for the clay's wet smile.

Twisting the lid tight,
I shoved the jar down,
palmed off my swift
profession of days
to the Dopplers of fall.
By increments, rain
stole through the lid
and burst each word's
sure star of insight,
and the hands that held
my names to the earth
raveled in the wind.
Let the jar crack and list
with the continent's drift,
I said and sailed past
the trash-flecked river
and cold brick towns
and moved fast over
the homes and trees.

www.ingramcontent.com/pod-product-compliance
Lightning Source LLC
Chambersburg PA
CBHW020943090426
42736CB00010B/1243